Harry Milles Fenn

The Vision of Misery Hill

A Legend of the Sierra Nevada and miscellaneous Verse

Harry Milles Fenn

The Vision of Misery Hill
A Legend of the Sierra Nevada and miscellaneous Verse

ISBN/EAN: 9783743349568

Manufactured in Europe, USA, Canada, Australia, Japa

Cover: Foto ©ninafisch / pixelio.de

Manufactured and distributed by brebook publishing software (www.brebook.com)

Harry Milles Fenn

The Vision of Misery Hill

Univ. of California
Withdrawn

THE LIBRARY OF THE
UNIVERSITY OF CALIFORNIA
DAVIS

THE VISION OF MISERY HILL

A LEGEND OF THE SIERRA NEVADA

AND

MISCELLANEOUS VERSE

BY

MILES I'ANSON

WITH ILLUSTRATIONS BY HARRY FENN
AND OTHERS

G. P. PUTNAM'S SONS
NEW YORK   LONDON
27 WEST TWENTY-THIRD ST.   27 KING WILLIAM ST., STRAND
The Knickerbocker Press
1891

INTRODUCTION.

To my fellow-miners of California and the Pacific Coast I inscribe this little book of verse, in memory of Auld Lang Syne and the land that hath so glamoured us; for though the themes herein are few that touch your peculiar life and environment, they were born of the high Sierras, and the desert solitudes near and far, during the arduous years and lonely hours of a gold-seeker's life.

Not in self-confidence, however, does the writer present these desultory utterances to you, but conscious how little of worth there is here to warrant the offering,—how little indeed of aught to portray such an experience and communion with Nature.

The writer has no thought of touching any popular chord in these conceits, nor hope beyond pleasing a few here and there ; and so,

"With a heart for any fate"—

as befits the Prospector—whatever of adverse judgment or of failure may greet this venture, will fall lightly upon him, as upon one inured to long-familiar loads.

THE AUTHOR.

NEWARK, NEW JERSEY,
June, 1891.

CONTENTS.

	PAGE
THE VISION OF MISERY HILL	1
REFLECTIONS ON A FOSSIL SHELL	34
WHERE ALICE IS	45
THE RAINY SEASON	47
LOVE'S PRESAGE	50
TO ANE THE CYNIC SOUGHT	51
THE OWL	54
MAMMON'S IN MEMORIAM	56
A VERNAL INVOCATION	67
LINES TO FLORENCE	68
COUNSEL FROM SOL. SLOWBOY	69
THE DEVIL'S WELL	74
INGERSOLL	88
FLIGHT BEYOND FAITH	89
DOUBT	90
THE CREED OF HOPE	91
THE GOSPEL O' GAMMON	97

CONTENTS.

	PAGE
PROGRESS—LIBERTY—DELUSION	102
HER DAYS OF JOY	107
FRANK FORESTER	109
ENCHANTMENT	111
IN ALTAS SIERRAS	112
THE FINAL REBELLION	119
IN MEMORIAM—CAPTAIN WEBB	126
UTTERANCE OF THE DESERT	131
THE ETERNAL SIEGE	133
ON HEARING A DESERT SONG-BIRD	140
HIS EPITAPH—TOM BLOSSOM OF ARIZONA	142
NIGHT-FALL ON THE YUBA	144

ILLUSTRATIONS.

	PAGE
"TOM BOWERS MINED ON MISERY HILL" .	2
"A HAND HE SAW STRETCHED LIKE A CLAW" .	26
"HE SPEEDS O'ER REALMS THAT SEEM ACCURST"	76
"A STRANGER AT THE DEVIL'S WELL" .	84
"HOW RANG OUR JOYFUL PEAL"	114
NIGHT-FALL ON THE YUBA	144

THE VISION OF MISERY HILL:

A LEGEND OF PIKE CITY, IN THE SIERRA NEVADA.

PART I.

Tom Bowers mined on Misery Hill,
    All round it and across it,—
Pursued for years with stubborn will
    His theories of deposit.

Tom's mind was fashion'd in the mould
    Of positive conviction,
That clutch'd belief with rigid hold,
    And scouted contradiction.

His mission was (he had no doubt)
    To trace the primal sources
Of all the gold once mined about
    The flats and water-courses;

And though the gold he gather'd there
  Was hardly worth the gaining,
"Whar this kem from"—thus reason'd Tom—
  "Thar must be more remaining."

And so he tunnell'd and he sluiced,
  He ditched and delved and drifted,
Till all the ground for acres round
  Was fairly search'd and sifted;

Till all the gulches and the slopes
  With prospect-holes were pitted,—
Sad graves, alas, of cherish'd hopes
  That one by one had flitted!

But tho' his work so futile seemed,
  None knew his faith to falter;
The miner tribe might jeer and gibe,
  His views they ne'er could alter.

The miner tribe might jeer and gibe,—
  He held the tribe mistaken;
The hidden lode was real to him
  As daily beans and bacon.

"TOM BOWERS MINED ON MISERY HILL"

Thus faith, tho' but a dream, is blest
  To all who toil or suffer;
Such faith, I hold, is more than gold,
  And all that wealth can offer.

And so in many a lone ravine
  Far lost to human neighbors,
Self-banished to his solitude
  Some digger lives and labors;—

The gnome of certain hills or streams
  Renowned in golden annals,
That seeks, in monomaniac dreams,
  His hidden veins and channels.

So, cabin'd on a lone divide
  Between the creek and canyon,
Tom lived and wrought, nor ever sought
  A partner or companion;

Nor yearned he for the outer world,
  Its busy strife and clamor;
This vagrant independent life
  Had spell'd him with its glamour,

And love of nature.—Thus he grew
   A man of lonely habit,
That all the secret coverts knew
   Of grizzly, grouse, and rabbit.

But ne'er a thing on foot or wing
   Had cause to flee or fear him;
The friendly quail beset his trail,
   The chipmonk gambol'd near him.

His presence frighted not the hare,
   Nor stopt the grouse's drumming;
The shyest creature lurking there
   Scarce startled at his coming;

Thus bold by frequence of his step,—
   His coming and his going;
Or theirs some finer sense, mayhap,
   To know beyond our knowing:

For peradventure every soul
   Hath some distinctive essence,—
Some fine, far-reaching aureole
   Of good or evil presence,

Impalpable to grosser sense,
  And visual cognition,
That wakes with subtle influence
  The watch-dog—Intuition.

And so he lived through fleeting years,
  Of worldly life unwitting,
With phantom hope still beckoning,
  With fortune ever flitting;

With few to know and none to share
  His daily hopes and sorrows,
Till time and toil had blanch'd his hair,
  And plough'd his face with furrows.

Time was, when to this plodding gnome
  Came missives sad and tender,
With news of far-off friends and home,
  And tokens of the sender:

These urged him back to ties of old,
  To love grown weary-hearted;
And their cessation sadly told
  Of hope or life departed;

For many a year had joined the past
  Since loving heart had spoken;
Neglect had conquer'd faith at last,—
  The final link was broken!

O! you who wander far a-west
  With high ambition burning—
Remember aye the loving breast
  That pines for your returning!

Wait not the prize ye may attain
  On some too-late to-morrow,—
Go now, and cheer that heart again,
  Ere life is closed in sorrow!

Though ties were sunder'd, home resign'd
  For this lone sanctuary,
Tom was no hater of his kind,
  No cynic solitary;

But promptly as the Sunday came
  He ceased his usual labors,—
Left solitude and issued thence
  To meet his mining neighbors.

He donn'd his better clothes that day;
　He baked and washed and mended,
And to "The Camp" some miles away
　O'er hill and canyon wended,

To take a social glass or two,
　To bandy joke and query,
And ask of aught discover'd new,
　And air his ancient the'ry

About the "lead" of Misery Hill,—
　Show where old Jenkins struck it,
And where he 'd find the channel still,
　With nuggets by the bucket.

And warming to his theme—perhaps
　Misled with mock attention—
Chalked on the floor impromptu maps
　To aid their comprehension.

Then some would wink and say, "I pass!"
　Some gibe him, rudely jolly,
While others roared, with lifted glass:
　"Here 's luck to Bowers' Folly!"

Tom wisely took but little heed
 Of such good-natured banter;
He knew their worst of word and deed
 Was born of the decanter.

Yet, on occasion, held his ground
 Against some trenchant joker;
Mayhap made answer—pointing round
 The bar and games of poker:

"Well, boys, some folks air out o' plumb,
 And p'raps my head aint level;
But what's the end o' keerds an' rum?—
 The boneyard and the devil!"

So passed the years with little change
 Or luck for Tom's behoovement;
But punctual in his narrow range
 As planetary movement,

He kept his even-gaited way,
 Still full of hope and vigor,
Till one tempestuous winter day
 The gaunt familiar figure

Came not to camp, and wonder grew
  To know what hap delayed him;
Snow blocked the trail and fierce the gale,
  But this had never stayed him.

And when the morrow brought him not,
  Nor yet the day succeeding,
Ten men of brawn, next day at dawn,
  With stout Jim Brandon leading,

Broke trail through drifting snows across
  The wintry desolation,
O'er rugged steep and canyon deep
  To Tom's lone habitation;

Where he, the guest of solitude,
  Had dwelt full many a winter;
Whence issued now no welcome smoke,
  No voice to bid them enter.

The hearth was cold, and knew no more
  The back-log brightly burning;
An outward track led from the door,
  But there was none returning!

And save his cat, that greeted them
  With mews and wistful purring,
No sign of life was round the place,
  Nor other creature stirring.

So thence the moody cavalcade
  The trail and footprints follow'd;
And mocking winds sole answer made
  Whene'er they paused and hallo'd.

And fierce the wintry tempest blew;
  The rugged way grew steeper;
The guiding traces fainter grew
  In snow-drifts gath'ring deeper;

While oft with vibrant shock and sound,
  Like mountains rent asunder,
Some giant pine, hurl'd earthward, drown'd
  The canyon's muffled thunder.

And grimmer lines marked every face
  With deeper doubting, fearing,
As grew the thought that he they sought
  Was past all help and hearing.

Then up the slopes of Grizzly Run,
  And thence by Deadwood Hollow
To Misery Hill they toiled, and still
  The trail was plain to follow;

Till up a deep and narrow cleft
  Where beetling banks impended,
There led the track, and then, alack!
  All trace abruptly ended!

For there where Tom had lately toiled,
  The treach'rous bank had slidden;
And well they knew what there from view
  That merciless mass had hidden!

And all stood silent and aghast,—
  Each face the story speaking;—
Poor Tom had struck the "lead" at last
  Beyond all earthly seeking!

Then tenderly and tearfully
  Those rugged men exhumed him;
And tenderly and carefully
  Thence bore him and entomb'd him,

Upon a little bed-rock knoll
   Beneath the waving spruces,
To dream no more of fabulous ore,
   Of channels, drifts, and sluices.

PART II.

Thenceforth for years the Bowers Claim
   Was neither worked nor wanted;
Tom's diggings had an evil name;
   Some vowed the Hill was haunted.

Nay, one who cross'd the Hill at night—
   Belated in the murk there—
Swore roundly that he saw a light,
   And heard Old Tom at work there!

But others jeered and ridiculed
   This tale of things uncanny;
Declared him fuddled or befool'd,
   And branded him "A granny."

Howbeit, miners shunn'd the ground
  As worthless or ill-fated,
And so for many a season round
  'T was bann'd and unlocated.

But passing years brought certain change,
  And paying claims grew fewer:
Prospecting took a wider range;
  Old claims were left for newer:

And so it happ'd that once again
  The ghostly Hill should waken
From deathful trance that one, perchance,
  Might earn his beans and bacon.

Jim Brandon, thriftless as of yore,
  And now a chronic debtor,
Forsook the claim that paid no more,
  And, delving 'round for better,

Strayed o'er the trail to Misery Hill,
  One drowsy day in summer;
Sat on the banks and mused awhile
  In retrospective humor;

Viewed all the work of fruitless years,—
  Tom's sluiceways, shafts, and ditches,—
The fatal cave and sudden grave
  That closed his dream of riches;

And o'er the acres ravaged there
  By that assiduous toiler,
Beheld how Nature's kindly care
  Had followed the despoiler,

To hide and heal each grievous wound
  By pick and torrent riven;
To fill the shafts and cave the drifts
  His hands had vainly driven.

Young pines and firs in vernal ranks
  The naked bed-rock shaded;
The creeping chickweed draped the banks
  And all the cuts invaded;

And many a slope of soil bereft,
  New vegetation nourished;
The spruce grew there and everywhere
  The manzanita flourished.

Jim thought—This ground is very poor,
   No doubt; but why pass by it
Like other fools?—He had the tools,
   And so resolved to try it.

He tested well the likely ground,
   And in the bottom gravel
Of Tom's last cut a prospect found,
   Which, past all doubt or cavil,

Would yield him half an ounce a day,—
   "Leastwise," he mused, "it oughter";
So clear'd for use the cumber'd sluice,
   And dug a ditch for water.

And things went better soon with Jim;
   He paid his debts, grew jolly,
And laugh'd with those who christen'd him
   "The Heir to Bowers' Folly."

But tho' so free and, as a rule,
   Good-natured and compliant,
Who wrong'd or play'd him for a fool
   Might 'rouse an angry giant.

And so it proved—for Jim of late
   Much temper had been showing
Against some wight who, in the night,
   Had set the water flowing

Through every sluice on Misery Hill,
   And which despite plain warning
How he might fare who trespass'd there,
   Was running every morning.

And when much bolder trespass still
   Upon the claim he noted,
His words, I wot, grew strong and hot,
   And cannot here be quoted.

A joke's a joke, thought Jim, but this
   Was push'd beyond all warrant;
And whether done in spite or fun
   Not yet to him apparent.

And vain his search in track or clue
   To find the raider hinted,
For, save his own, no foot was shown
   Upon the Hill imprinted.

Then, as the rogue so deftly came,
    Shunn'd daylight, and was wary,
Jim made resolve to watch the claim
    All night, if necessary.

So, broaching to his cabin-chum—
    Doc Sanders—his intention,
With caution to keep strictly mum,
    Nor give it hint or mention

To any soul in camp or town,—
    Not e'en to boon companions,—
He took his trusty rifle down
    And slipped across the canyons,

By devious ways and round about,
    To trap the rogue that trickt him,
And stealthy as a Pawnee scout
    Who would surprise his victim.

Jim's courage had been often tried;
    He faltered at no trifle;
No man more quick with axe or pick,
    None handier with the rifle.

All ghostly tales to him were jokes,
   And spirits sheer delusion;—
"They 'll do fer fools and women-folks,"
   Was Jim's concise conclusion.

Too full of strife his nomad life,
   Too hedged with hard conditions,
For metaphysics or the sway
   Of ancient superstitions;

All he had ever chance to learn
   Was rude and necessary;
And "his" was *his'n*, "hers" was *hern*,
   In Jim's vocabulary.

And so he strode to Misery Hill,
   With hope intenser growing
To catch the wight that every night
   Had set the water flowing.

But as one stalking wary game
   May neither haste nor loiter,
So travell'd he, till near the claim,
   Then paused to reconnoitre,

And saw—or was 't a trick of sight?—
  A strange, uncertain glimmer
Upon the Hill,—a lambent light,
  Now brighten, now grow dimmer;—

Such gleam as night on tropic seas
  Shows in each wave upturning;
Such light as lives in mouldering trees,
  Or glowworm bluely burning.

The nearer hills lay in eclipse
  Beneath the mountain masses;
Beyond, the white Sierra tips
  Shone o'er the shadow'd passes.

He heard within the tamaracks
  The night-wind's eerie crooning;
From bars and falls at intervals
  The Yuba's deep bassooning.

And every pine grew full of moan;
  The moon was in the crescent;
A "Notice" on a hemlock shown
  In letters phosphorescent.

THE VISION OF MISERY HILL.

"A mining notice!—Umph," growl'd Jim,
  "He wants a little fun here;—
He 'll get it" (and his face grew grim)
  "Before Jim Brandon's done here!"

With bated breath he read the name
  In lambent letters shining:
"*I, Thomas Bowers, hereby claim
  This ground for placer mining!*"

Then dash'd his hand in sudden ire
  To rend the lie there written;—
His hand fell from the words of fire
  As if with palsy smitten!

For this, in sooth, was something weird,—
  A sense of fear flash'd o'er him;
The mystic words had disappeared,—
  The tree stood blank before him!

"A trick!" he muttered through his teeth,
  As o'er the brushwood striding
He sought around, above, beneath,
  To find the culprit hiding;

But nothing living found or heard,
    Save here and there a cricket,
Or barking fox, or frightened bird
    That fluttered in the thicket;

Or haply, from his lonely height
    On pine-tree's lofty column,
An owl awoke the drowsy night
    With utterance deep and solemn.

Then o'er the hill Jim crept alert,
    No sound or sign discerning
Of him he sought, but overwrought
    With futile, passionate yearning,

Beat every covert far around,
    Through every thicket peering,
Until again the higher ground
    And mystic hemlock nearing—

Was 't fancy? or the rising wind
    Through forest branches blowing?
That surely meant to ears attent
    The sound of water flowing!

And lo, again in lines of flame
    Upon the tree was shining,—
"*I, Thomas Bowers, hereby claim
    This ground for placer mining!*"

Then while he stood with list'ning ear
    The mystery to unravel,
Up from the cut came sharp and clear
    A pick-stroke in the gravel.

Ay, there again!—his breath came quick;—
    So! there the scamp was lurking!
The rushing sluice and ringing pick
    Proclaimed a miner working!

As nimbly as a catamount
    Jim crouch'd to watch and listen;
You might have seen the savage sheen
    Within his eyeballs glisten!

Then to the bank edge, creeping slow,
    And through the brackens gazing,
He something saw that changed to awe
    The wrath within him blazing.

An eerie shape—too grim and lank
  To be a living creature's—
Full in the moon beneath the bank
  Upturned its ghastly features;

Moved lips that uttered not a sound,
  And raised a warning finger;
Jim fain had fled, but sudden dread
  Impell'd him there to linger.

Was this a phantom of the cup?
  A dreamer's horrent vision?
Nay, fancy never conjured up
  So real an apparition!

Too well he knew that grizzly beard,
  That visage wan and shrunken,
Those eyes that flamed with lustre weird
  From sockets deeply sunken!

But while he gazed, transfixed and dazed,
  Upon the phantom figure,
His finger half instinctively
  Reach'd out and touch'd the trigger.

The hammer fell . . . there came a yell
   That sent a spasm through him!
And from the gulf the spectre sprang
   With pick and shovel to him!

He tarried not, but fled the spot
   Where all was now unravell'd;
His iron-shodden miner shoes
   Struck fire as fast he travell'd.

He bounded lithely, wing'd with fear;
   His legs were ne'er so limber;
He cleared the ditches like a deer,
   He leapt the fallen timber;

And round the echoing rim of night
   His hasty steps resounded;
Three hollow clanks rang on the planks
   As o'er a bridge he bounded.

Then down the ridge to Bloody Gulch
   He madly dash'd and doubled,
Plunging with mighty strides across
   Its torrent red and troubled;

And up the hill where Burke's old mill
   Stood naked, roof and rafter,
Wherefrom a startled owlet shrill'd
   His wild, hysteric laughter,—

That seemed an impish hue and cry
   To Jim's excited fancy;
And things he knew so strangely grew,
   By some dread necromancy,

That every stump within his path
   Rose gorgon-like to hound him,
And ancient oaks in ghostly wrath
   Waved arms and gibber'd round him.

Solve you the riddle why this man
   Should flee in coward panic,
Who scarce had thought or fear of aught
   Celestial or satanic;—

This nomad, trained in border war,—
   A desperado branded,
Who track'd the grizzly to his lair,
   And slew him single-handed.

But thus he sped in nameless dread,
  How fast it little matter'd,
For close arear the thing of fear
  With pick and shovel clatter'd.

At last the camp lights came to view
  As, every sinew straining,
O'er Hoyt Divide he madly fled,
  New strength and courage gaining.

But ah!—just where his shadow fell,
  Shown by the moonlight clearer,
A hand he saw stretch'd like a claw
  That nearer drew and nearer!

PART III.

It was a gala night in "Pike,"—
  A night of rout and revel;
The "Dandy Jim" had made a strike
  Upon the second level.

"A HAND HE SAW STRETCH'D LIKE A CLAW"

Success had crowned the "Nip-and-tuck,"—
  The claim was now "a daisy";
And Gopher Sam had struck a vein
  That set The Camp half crazy.

In Jimson's Tamarack saloon
  The jubilation centr'd,
And from its door a mighty roar—
  When later comers enter'd—

Shot forth a sudden bolt of sound,
  That smote with mocking riot
The calm, majestic hills around,
  The night's impressive quiet.

Such strife within! such peace without!
  O man, thou errant creature—
The solemn hills return thy shout,
  And bid thee back to Nature!

So pure without! so foul within!
  And ever the air grew thicker,
And louder rose the frantic din
  As flowed the fiery liquor.

For there the roystering revellers—
    That all the week had fasted
From drink and play—had come to stay
    While gold or credit lasted ;—

Had come from hills and river-bars,
    From lone ravines and gorges,—
A hungry throng for dance and song,
    And bacchanalian orgies.

And round the games the circles grew
    Where favorite Poker spell'd them,
Or Faro's fascination drew,
    Or Spanish Montè held them.

And loudly buzzed the miner clan
    Of sluicing, drifting, ditching ;
Pete had a dollar to the pan ;
    Dick's bed-rock now was "pitching" ;

Tom Blossom still was " off the lead,"
    And barely earned his rations,
But yet, "by dad," he swore, he had
    " The best of indications."

Ay, it was ever thus with Tom,—
  And all his comrades knew it,—
He saw the prize before his eyes
  But never quite got to it!

And thousands fight with fate, alas,
  As luckless as poor Tom is!
Whose lives are blossom full, but pass
  Unknowing the fruit of promise!

A troupe of dancing-girls that late
  The Diggings had invaded,
Each with a graceless miner mate
  Now waltzed and gallopaded;

And up and down the bar-room whirl'd
  The rough, good-natured diggers,
While one forlorn flutina skirl'd
  The tunes and timed the figures.

But where was Jim—Jim Brandon?—he
  Whose welcome aye was hearty
At spree or dance, and ne'er by chance
  Had been an absent party?

The question 'rose and oft recurr'd
    Between the games and dances,
Till much opinion had been heard
    And each had aired his fancies;

Till o'er Jim's absence, and his claim,
    A few grew loud and heated,
When, from a quiet poker game
    Where he had long been seated,

Doc Sanders rose, with glass in hand:
    "Sho, boys!—(hic)—let's be jolly!—
Whar's Jim?—well (hic) here's luck to him!—
    He's—gone to—Bowers' Folly!"

The words he said had barely sped
    When, hark! a fearful clatter
Brought every reveller to his feet
    To question—What's the matter?

A crash of tools, a shout, a thud
    As of a body falling,
A yell that froze each hearer's blood—
    So piercing and appalling—

Came from without, and bold men felt
　　Their pulses strangely quicken;
And some, as when the Banshee cries,
　　Stood dumb and terror-stricken.

And for the moment features flushed
　　With drink and play grew pallid;
But some who dread nor quick or dead
　　Out from the bar-room sallied,—

Like men impatient of defence
　　When threat'ning foes beleaguer,
Who raise the port and madly thence
　　Make sortie swift and eager;

These led the wondering rabble forth,
　　To find no dead or dying,
As that dread cry might well imply,
　　But on the roadway lying,

Jim Brandon's rifle—known to all,
　　And, by the flaring candles,
A pick and shovel, with "T. B."
　　Cut rudely in the handles!

What did it mean ?   Was this the scene
   Of tragedy or juggle ?
Some tracks were found as if the ground
   Were tramp'd in desp'rate struggle—

And nothing more !   But what of Jim ?
   Nay, ask the sighing pines there !
No trace was ever found of him
   Beyond the tracks and signs there !

.   .   .   .

Long years have passed, and over all
   Young pines grow rank and vernal;
And still the claim hath evil name
   For sights and sounds nocturnal;

And miners swear—tho' buried there
   Beneath the waving spruces—
Tom Bowers still holds Misery Hill,
   And nightly runs the sluices.

REFLECTIONS ON A FOSSIL SHELL.

[On the lofty slopes of Volcano Mountain, in Esmeralda, Nevada, the writer chanced upon and prospected the shore-line of an ancient sea, finding its argentiferous shales poor in precious metal, but rife with fossil life-forms of the Silurian Age.]

Here in these dead and desert lands
  Of Nature's rudest moods and shapes,
  Of wrinkled peaks and weather'd capes
That loom from seas of burning sands,—

Where yet, as through unnumbered years,
  The stealthy-footed Pah Ute prowls,
  The lank coyotè weirdly howls
His hunger-woes to savage ears,—

How puny seems this humanite,
  That like a worm laborious creeps
  Upon the Vulcan-bowldered steeps!
See, far o'erhead in daring flight—

As if in utter scorn of him—
   An eagle soar; and leagues below,
   Where solar heats concentr'd glow
On shimmering mesas vast and dim—

Look down through airy gulfs and trace
   A filament as finely spun
   As spider's web shine in the sun,—
Man's highest triumph over space,

Where he hath drawn the iron bands
   O'er which his Van of Progress drives,
   That bind in firm, fraternal gyves,
Far alien, antipodean lands.

From rocky spurs that run athwart
   These drear Saharas of the West,—
   Where, toiling in their madding quest,
The treasure-seekers grim and swart

Disrupt the flinty strata—lo!
   By hammer-stroke from age-long night
   This ancient shell leapt into light
With message of the Long Ago,—

When embryonic life began,
   That forth in crude essayings crept;
   When Thought in lowly creatures slept,
Ere waking to its growth in Man.

How vain, O Science, thy computes
   Of Time since roar of ancient seas
   Awoke reverb'rant voice in these
Ensealed and silent convolutes!

We sound the Past with idle guess,—
   Reach o'er the gulf our yard-stick gauge;
   We prate of Epoch and of Age,
And dream we mete the measureless!

Yet, while I held within my hand
   This ancient creature's crumbling shell,—
   Behold!—as by some wizard spell
Old Time's tenebr'ous gulf was spann'd!

And I beheld a scene of dread,
   To sentient being ne'er shown before,—
   The waste and inchoate world of yore
In awful desolation spread!

REFLECTIONS ON A FOSSIL SHELL.

Where o'er the dumb, pre-natal sleep
 Of Nature hung the mists of morn,
 And continents lay newly born
Upon the dark, perturbèd deep.

No life above the sombre seas;
 Not yet a bird or beast—alas!
 Not yet the firstling blade of grass
Was born of Nature's alchemies!

From zone to zone on shallow strands
 I heard the drear sea-surges beat;
 And through a nebulous winding-sheet
The sun cast o'er the lifeless lands

A weirdly-dim, penumbral light,
 As when volcanic forces shroud
 The firmament with ashen cloud,
And day seems glooming into night.

Strange power was mine; at will I pass'd
 Across the dreary seas and lands;
 I called aloud with lifted hands
Through soundless solitudes, aghast

At my own voice, which seemed not mine,
    But some lost creature's hopeless cry;
    Yet ne'er from pitiless earth or sky
Came life's response in sound or sign!

So sped amain in sore affright
    Through Day's dim-litten zones, and where
    Tartarean fires with baleful glare
Illumin'd the sable breast of Night;

Where raged in sulphurous canopies,
    Dread storms of elemental war,
    And never light of moon or star,
Nor glimmer of the Pleiades

Proclaimed the peopled firmament;
    But muffled in her murky robe
    Earth seemed a lost and wandering globe,
Of starless space sole habitant.

Still onward, urged by fear profound,
    To blank horizons never past,
    But ever opening void and vast
On Desolation's wider bound!

Where yet upon the plastic sphere
　The shadow of the Maker's hand
　Seemed moving, and from sea and land
Reverb'd His thunders to the ear!

O Soul! it were a fate accurst
　To be the last upon the earth!
　But unto being of human birth
A fate more dread to be the first!

To walk alone such world as this,
　Still lifeless from the gulf of space,—
　The far forerunner of his race,
So near creation's genesis!

Thus ran my thought, and horror grew,
　Till borne upon the sudden wings
　Grim Fancy to a dreamer brings,
Out from that ancient world I flew

As from a nightmare's hideous thrall,
　With joyful cry to be again
　So near the cheery haunts of men
Upon my lofty mountain wall;

To be within the Human Age,
   And part of that supernal plan
   Which gives the ripened Earth to man,
And Life's supremest heritage.

How glorious seemed the earth and sky!
   It was a blessèd thing to see
   A wrinkled lizard near to me
With keen cognition in his eye!

And e'en the bristling cactus, rife
   With venom'd spines, benignant grew
   To soul so grateful to renew
The joyful fellowship of life.

O waif from Time's unmeasured sea!
   Are we that question sky and earth,
   With mighty hope of higher birth,
By some far link allied to thee?

Alas! are these supernal powers
   The fruitage of some soulless germ?
   Is that which animates the worm
A living force divine as ours?

Creed answers nay, but Science saith
   Dumb predecessor such as this
   May type the homely chrysalis
From which such beauty blossometh.

It better suits our faith and pride
   To hold that, nobly-fashioned thus,
   We leapt at Word Miraculous
Divinely-imaged, God-allied.

Yet surely miracle as great
   Marks every growth of life and thought,
   And all creative law hath wrought
From humble unto higher state.

Though fact with faith may not align,
   Or prove a fin became a claw,
   The claw a hand, beneath the law,
Is this creation less divine?

Nay, though these riper faculties
   Did blossom from no finer dust
   Than this poor waif—yet shall we trust
That faiths are more than phantasies:

That since one law supremely reigns
   Alike for embryo and man,
   No life is lost where it began,
But ever moves to higher planes.

And if there were no farther scope
   For Him that built this house of lime,
   And kindred life, through endless time,
A shadow falls upon our hope:

Then yonder lights in heaven's abyss
   Are meteors in eternal gloom,
   And Being bears the awful doom—
Thou art this thing, and only this!

Yea, all is blank, inscrutable!
   A gulf behind, a gulf before,
   And Life is cast for evermore
In rigid mould, immutable!

What do we peril if we look
   Through God's domain with microscopes?
   Shall some dread Finis bar our hopes
Who seek His ways beyond The Book?

Fear not! for every seeker knows
    How vain the Ultimate is sought,—
    How vaster to the flight of thought
God's universe forever grows.

But whoso leaves the land before
    He knows the port to which he sails,
    May drift despairing in the gales
And restful harbor find no more!

So, anchor by the faith thou hast,
    Secure within thy placid pond,
    While doubters roam the deeps beyond,
Or sink with shatter'd helm and mast.

And this mute witness of the time
    When Earth was creeping through the haze
    Of newness to these riper days
Of life and growth, and thought sublime,

May teach us, though his lips be dumb,
    To trust in faith the kindly Power
    That shaped us to the present hour
And limns the higher life to come;—

That Nature,—working out the plan
   Whose boundaries we are fain to set,—
   Works onward, not senescent yet,
Nor all her powers exhaust in Man.

And while Polemics hold debate
   On God's creation,—thus, or so,—
   Suffice it thou and I to know—
Not how, but that He Does Create.

WHERE ALICE IS.

Come with me, O charming maid,
To the forest's vernal shade
  Where no strife or malice is,
And no cares of life invade;—
  Peace shall reign where Alice is!

Come and seek the Dryad's home
  In the wildwood trellises;
Or by ocean's roar and foam
Blithely let us live and roam;—
  Joy shall reign where Alice is!

Come where lilies, blossoming,
  Lift their fragrant chalices
To each living, loving thing
Pulsing with the life of Spring;
  Love shall reign where Alice is!

So like Elfin king and queen,
Monarchs of a blest demesne,
Throned in leafy palaces
Love and Joy and Peace, I ween,
Shall be mine and Alice's!

THE RAINY SEASON.

In deeper shadows fell the gloom
Within the lonely cabin's room
   Where two old miners fared ;
One sat against the chimney side
In silence, while the embers died,
   And one for sleep prepared,—
Still chattering blithely to his dumb,
Disheartened, melancholy chum,
Of better days and luck to come
   With dawn of the Rainy Season.

He called his mate—yet brooding there
Beside the hearth's departing glare—
   " Ho, comrade ! wake and hear
The roaring pines and stormy blast
Proclaiming summer o'er at last,
   The rainy season near !

THE RAINY SEASON.

The rain, the rain, the blessèd rain,
That brings the harvest to the plain,
And yellow gold from gulch and vein :
  Hurrah for the Rainy Season !

"Though grub be scant, and credit gone,
And claims have petered one by one—
  Away with doubt and fear !
We 've built the flume and dug the ditch ;
The gravel in Red Ravine is rich ;
  And hark !—the rain is here !
The rain, the rain, the joyful rain
Now beats the cabin roof amain
Till every shingle rings again :
  Hurrah for the Rainy Season !

"Cheer up !—we 'll strike the channel yet !
And Bill, old boy, you can't forget
  Our ups and downs together,
Through many a hardship, many a miss ;—
But you—you never gave up like this,
  Nor flinched at work or weather !

And now the rain, the bounteous rain
Is pouring down on peak and plain,
Till ranch and mine rejoice again:
　　Hurrah for the Rainy Season!

"Come, partner, shake your gloomy mood,
Nor longer o'er misfortune brood,
　　But let the past be past;
D' ye hear the tempest shake the door?
The canyon's rising waters roar?
　　Success is near at last!"—
But ah! he called his mate in vain,
For Death had come before the rain!
And Bill would never respond again,
　　Nor toil in the Rainy Season!

LOVE'S PRESAGE.

O sad-eyed mother, dropping tears
    O'er cherub cheek and rosy limb!
Thy loving fears forebode the years
    That reach remorseless hands for him!—
For him, sweet babe, that from his nest
    Looks wonder at thy sudden grief,
Nor dreams his rest upon thy breast
    Shall be, ah me, so passing brief!

But time will take, for ill or good,
    Each darling from the mother's knee;
And soon thy bud of babyhood
    Must blossom to depart from thee!
Yet, though he roam to farthest clime,
    Though grief and shame his steps attend,—
Though red with crime, thy love sublime
    Will find and fold him to the end!

TO ANE THE CYNIC SOUGHT.

O thou, whase honest nature spurns
The guilty wage that baseness earns,
The gainful lie, the fat returns
   O' fraud and wrang,—
For thee, puir saul, a bardie mourns
   In heart and sang!

Thy tender conscience is a gift
Forbidding hope o' warldly thrift;
Och! better thou wert sense bereft,
   Or black mischance
Had cast thee, Pariah-like, adrift
   On life's expanse!

Integrity 's a fossil weed
To a' this modern Mammon greed,—
A thing lang dead to ken and need
   Ayont the name:

The paukie tongue and pliant creed
  Are wealth and fame!

Nae wonner, friend, that hands recoil
Frae sawing sticks and tilling soil,
When ane wi' knackit to despoil
  A bank or twa,
May snap his thumbs at honest toil
  For ance and a'!

And Justice—hoot! the venal minx
Can see as weel's a hungry lynx!
Attend her coort when siller clinks
  For Crœsus' sins,
And mark the hizzie's nods and winks
  While siller wins!

But when your paltry fingers itch—
Wee pilf'ring rogue or famished wretch—
Tak tent!—she'll hound ye to the ditch
  Whase theft a crust is!
Gae steal a million, man, and clutch
  The scales o' Justice!

TO ANE THE CYNIC SOUGHT.

This life 's a game that maist beginners
Maun learn thro' dool and scrimpit dinners,
While sleekit knaves the trumps and winners
   Full-handed haud,
And praising fools and fellow-sinners
   Their tricks applaud.

But thou, wha toils in honest ways,
May moil and hunger a' thy days,
And fleech and snool for bread an' claes
   On supple knee,—
Nae wardly prize nor fellow praise
   For sic as thee!

Yet, friend, I 'll wad my aith upon 't—
Though scouted here and pinched wi' want—
There is for thee a place ayont
   Auld Charon's beck,
Where Peter waits to ca' thee saunt,
   And lift the sneck!

THE OWL.

He loves his lonely ivied nook
    Far up the old gray wall,
Whence his unlidded eyes may look
    Unseen, yet seeing all ;
He loves the moon's uncanny light ;
He hoots his joy when starless night
    Hath draped her dunnest pall ;
But like a guilty soul, doth shun
The searching eye of noonday sun !

By graveyard paths and haunted ways,
    When half the world 's asleep,
He sees with fixed, unfearful gaze
    The shapes of evil creep ;
Or from his ancient oak espies
The fateful tryst, the sacrifice,
    The lost that walk and weep :

THE OWL.

O bird, that sittest grim and still,
I fear thou art colleagued with ill!

And thou dost typify to me
　His nature, stern and grim,
Whose heart ne'er melts in sympathy,
　Whose eyes no tears bedim;
Who sits aloof with stony stare
While sorrow darkens to despair,
　And Misery pleads to him!
But wrapped in self, as with a cowl—
" Tu-whit! tu-hoo!"—what cares the owl!

MAMMON'S IN MEMORIAM.

AT THE CEMETERIES, "LONE MOUNTAIN," SAN FRANCISCO.

O strong young empire, marching free!
At last by this Hesperian sea,
The bivouac-halt is blown for thee.

Thy tents are pitched, thy march is done;
Behind thee lies the guerdon won;
Before, the sea and setting sun.

Here, where Pacific's thunderous waves
Resound from headland cliffs and caves—
Behold a hundred thousand graves!

The fallen of an army, these,
That swarmed from Earth's antipodes,
From northern lands and tropic seas;

From every clime and race enrolled;—
An army of the strong and bold,
Recruited at the cry of "Gold!"

And lo! as if by fairy planned,
A city crowns the hills of sand,
And fleets blow in from every land.

Here sweep the winds from western zones,
Fog-laden, voiceful with the moans
Of surges round the Farallones,

That landward run their course of fate—
Alas, like many a soul elate,
Here fallen at the Golden Gate!

O sea, that blows such doleful breath
O'er all these acres sown with death!—
What is 't thy sorrowing spirit saith?

Sweet Peace is here, and Strife is dumb;
The turmoils of the city come
No louder than the beetle's hum;

But Sorrow cometh here to shed
Her secret tears, and kindly spread
Fresh flowers above her sainted dead.

For her thy wild sea-pipers blow
Their coronachs, and loud and low
Sound every chord of human woe!

O realm of peace, and death, and flowers!
How dear to thought in vagrant hours
Thy labyrinthine paths and bowers!

What joy, these spring-in-winter days,
To flee the world's soul-fettering ways
And dream within thy brambly maze!

To watch the rabbits play, and hear
The friendly quail afar and near,
From shadowy thickets piping clear!

Here let us walk, for all the air
Is sweet with shrubs; exotics rare
Their aromatic burdens bear;

And man and art with nature vie
To mask with pleasance from the eye
The coffined host that round us lie.

One coverlet o'er all is spread
That sleep within this common bed,
And class, and caste, and pride are dead!

—Are dead? Nay, to the dead alone:
For Wealth still barriers from her own
The pauper and the poor unknown;

Still bans them to the wastes and holes,
And proudly from her templed knolls
O'erlooks the dust of common souls!

Here soars the high memorial shaft
To base success and worldly craft,
By Flattery duly epitaphed;

And yonder, through acacia blooms,
A regal mausoleum looms
Superbly o'er the stately tombs,

Bronze-gated and with gilt aflame.—
Draw near, and read what honored name
Great deeds have bruited into fame.

Is this the shrine of one who fought
For others' weal, or nobly wrought
To broaden human life and thought?

Sleeps here some laurel'd bard or sage?
Some patriot heart that cast the gage
To tyrants and redeemed his age?

Or one who, sceptered with the pen,
Still holds in deathless love and ken
His kingship o'er the minds of men?

Nay, friend, none such! yet o'er this mould
The blazoned tablet might have told,
" Here lies a king—the king of Gold."

A king not born to regal state,
But, sooth, a puissant potentate
And arbiter of human fate;

Whose glamoured subjects madly ran
To serve, or trumpet in his van—
" Behold, O world, this self-made man ! "

Whose dire Mephistophelian art
Taught multitudes the gamester's part,
And snared them in the gilded mart!

For well he knew the ruling trait—
This king !—and how to operate
His fool-traps set with golden bait!

Alike to shrewd and simple showed
The road to wealth (a royal road !)
That led through his Bonanza Lode.

And thousands entered, thousands fell !—
Alas ! alas ! and proved it well—
The very Arch-fiend's road to hell.

. . . . . .

The loiterers that gather here
Come not to honor or revere,
Nor bless these ashes with a tear;

But to all fellow-feeling lost,
With critic eyes appraise the cost
Of shrining this ignoble dust.

Saith one: "Here rests the busy brain
Of him that plann'd with might and main,
Insatiate still in greed of gain;

"Who, reaping past his utmost need,
Gave back the liberal Earth no seed
Of fruitful thought or noble deed;

"Whose thrift was like the deadly blight
Of some portentous parasite,
Grown rank on stolen life and light!"

Another: "Ay, here Mammon died
And built his fane, wherein are pride
And sordid lust self-glorified!

"Here worldly honors, thickly sown
In pomp, and art, and chisel'd stone,
Are his—who lived for self alone;

"While all around us modest Worth,
Through life-long failure, dole and dearth,
Returns unmarked to mother Earth!

"The wealth that shrines this worthless clay
Might show Despair the cheerful day,
And fright the hunger-wolf away

"From many a wretched chimney-side
Where Penury sits hollow-eyed,
And famished mouths the crumbs divide!"

Oh, shall a specious Latin phrase
Forbid reproach of evil ways,
And death beguile us into praise?

Nay, let the truth or nought be said!
He adds no honor to the dead
Who carves a lie above his head;

Else shall our lives and graves attest
That honor lies in lucre-quest,
And to be base is to be blessed!

If Death's alembic purifies
From earthly dross, and souls grown wise
Survey their past with sadden'd eyes ;—

Or, flitting from some higher sphere,
On loving missions hover near
To watch our lives, to warn and cheer,—

This soul, transfigured from the vault,
Would bid the glozing chisel halt
And blazon his besetting fault.

O dust of life so desolate!
Nor sculptured stone nor brazen gate
Can rank thee with the good and great!

Nay, though thy pride and wealth out-bid
The builder of the pyramid,
Oblivion guards thy coffin-lid;

And yon poor Nameless wrapped in sod,—
O'er whom the wind-sown grasses nod,—
Is nearer unto man and God!

But hadst thou rightly understood
The bonds of human brotherhood,
How blest thy life had been for good!

Not thine the honorable spoil
The useful arts may yield to toil
From mart and workshop, sea and soil:

O scorner of the honest bread!—
Thou, like a bird that beaks the dead,
On human frailty grossly fed!

Thy arts robbed Plenty of her store,
Drove Thrift to beggary, nor forbore
To prey on Want, and grasp for more!

Thy arts turned joy to hopeless grief;
Made life-long probity a thief,
And mad self-murder blest relief!

So stands the record;—read it, knaves,
In cells where dread unreason raves;
In blighted homes and early graves!

So stands the record, deeply scored
In living hearts! And his reward?—
This stone-heap, and a futile hoard.

Pause here, O ye whose eager grip
Lets not the miser'd treasure slip
Till death revokes your stewardship!

Break, break in life your mammon-gyves!
Nor hope to sanctify base lives
With liberal gold when death arrives.

Alas! the late post-mortem gift
Can never the sordid soul uplift
To earthly love or heavenly shrift!

A VERNAL INVOCATION.

Soar, skylark, to the azure dome,
And call the truants back that roam ;
　From southward groves, O bluebird, hasten !
Come, robin, unto thy northern home.

Pour forth your blithest roundelay,
O birds, to incense-breathing May !
　And o'er the quicken'd zones rejoicing,
Hail Nature's new resurrection day.

Now once again the woodlands ring
With song, and wondrous blossoming
　From Winter's tenebrific slumber
Proclaims the miracle of the Spring.

So, Soul, when thy worn garment lies
In graveyard mould, mayst thou arise,
　And from the dust benignly blossom
To glorious life in heavenly skies !

LINES TO FLORENCE.

There comes with Summer's bloom and leaf,
   A joyful thing that gayly speeds
   On gorgeous wings through flowery meads,
Unvexed with care or grief;—

A bright and dainty fugitive
   That nought unclean contaminates,
   Nor sullied with the lusts and hates
That mar the lives we live.

Be thine, dear child, such lot as this,—
   Not idle, but as free from care
   As this bright blossom of the air,
As sinless in thy bliss!

COUNSEL FROM SOL. SLOWBOY.

My plodding friend, break loose and send
    Your treadmill bonds to blazes!
Go kick your heels in clover fields,
    And roll among the daisies!

Let day-books go to Jericho!
    De'il take the price of tallow!
Yon grassy banks will rest your shanks,
    And let your brain lie fallow.

The wise are they who every day
    Enjoy life as it passes,
And carol still through good or ill;
    The rest, I fear, are asses!

Now, let us see—you 're forty-three,
    And though your eye still twinkles,
Old Time and Care have touched your hair,
    And sketched the coming wrinkles.

'T is time to rest from lucre-quest—
  "*Too poor?*" nay, that's mere gammon!
You've ample wealth for peace and health,
  And moderate love of Mammon.

"*Your business?*"—tut! you're in a rut
  Worn deep in self-delusion,
And year by year trot round in fear
  Of ruin and confusion.

But after you and I are through
  With profits, debts, and taxes,
The world, no doubt, will turn about
  As usual, on its axis;

And when we're gone some other one
  Will do as well as we did,—
For time and Fate, O friend, but wait
  To fill our shoes when needed!

"*Your children?*"—well, there's lazy Belle,
  Tom (junior), Maude, and Jerry;
But why should they have all the play,
  And you the work and worry?

Yet, day by day you plod away,
  Ignoring soul and body,
While Belle (vain lass!) is at her glass,
  And Tom—is at his toddy!

And thus, old friend, the shadowed end
  Appeals and bids you ponder!
Is 't wise to slave and scrimp and save
  That idle heirs may squander?

Wealth got by will is rife with ill—
  Ay, worse than want to many!
Make children earn, and thereby learn
  The worth of every penny.

That 's why I say, Go forth and play,
  Enjoy life while it passes,
Thus saving less for idleness,
  May save your lads and lasses.

Let 's look ahead.—When you are dead
  Then comes the usual jangle;
Unheard-of heirs contend for shares,
  And hungry lawyers wrangle.

One wife we knew, nor dreamed of *two*,
    But death brings strange surprises,
And now, to claim your honor'd name—
    Lo, number two arises!

Blackmail, of course! tho' something worse
    Is hinted—but, no matter,—
Wealth always draws the hawks and daws
    To peck the dead, and chatter!

Your intellect was doubtless wrecked,—
    A fact more sad than funny!
For it is found they 're seldom sound
    Who die and leave much money!

And so your will, though drawn with skill,
    Provokes a mighty rumpus,
And experts swear, and courts declare
    You clearly were *non compos*.

Then, when at last the strife is past,
    And wrangling ends in revel,
Belle weds some fraud and goes abroad,
    And Tom goes to—the devil!

And ere again the summer rain
  Brings daisies to the meadow,
Some wiser chap has won, mayhap,
  Your still attractive widow!

And so I say, Be wise to-day,—
  Enjoy life's cheery phases,
And carol still through good or ill,
  And roll among the daisies!

THE DEVIL'S WELL.

PRELUDE.

They passed the threshold in their prime,—
   Three stalwart sons were they,
That from their lowly cottage door
   One morn at break of day,
With tearful eyes but hopeful hearts,
   Rode westward and away.

And there were two left desolate
   Within the village lane,—
A wretched pair that gazed adieu
   Through Sorrow's blinding rain,
And cried aloud, " God bless our boys,
   And guide them home again !"

Then months grew into years, and Death
   Came with his summons stern ;

And one who stood within the lane
  Left one alone to mourn;
And long the widow'd mother sighed—
  "O sons of mine, return!"

Low sinks the fierce and fervent sun,
  Where mountains looming vast
On Arizona's torrid plains
  Their giant shadows cast;
And from a dark arroyo's mouth
  A horseman rideth fast.

Why spurs this courier o'er the waste
  Thus at the close of day,
With rifle poised and eye alert
  As if for sudden fray?
He bears the Mail to lonely camps
  A hundred miles away.

But wherefore sweeps his searching eye
  The scene so wild and drear,—

So silent all and desolate
  The peace of death seems here?
Sure, nought but guilt or coward heart
  Could dream of danger near.

No craven he: that rugged form
  In tawny buckskin dight,
Bears heart within as bold and true
  As e'er did ancient knight;
That hand the fierce Apache slew
  In many a bloody fight.

And well he knows the treach'rous peace
  Who rides here undismayed,—
Knows life must hold the citadel
  With ready shot and blade
For lurking outlaw, savage guile,
  And deadly ambuscade.

He speeds o'er realms that seem accurst
  By some malignant ban,
Where savage Nature scorns the weak,
  And leagued with savage man,

"HE SPEEDS O'ER REALMS THAT SEEM ACCURST"

Maintains a rigorous reign, and he
  May keep his life who can.

Where bleaching bones of man and beast
  Mark Slaughter's cruel sway,
And graveless lie the fallen dead
  To feast the birds of prey,
Or mummy there in desert air
  And grimly waste away.

But scathless he had lived and fought
  Through scenes of blood and woe,
While one ill-fated brother fell
  In ambush years ago;
The other roams for vengeance yet,
  And death to the savage foe.

His broncho is a trusty beast,
  That ne'er was known to fail
In wind or speed when urgent need
  Bade flight upon the trail;
Nor ever flinched at rifle-shot,
  Or shied at sudden assail.

And all her rider's will she knows,
　　Each word and touch obeys;
Can keep the trail in blackest night
　　Through wild, untravelled ways
And shun the yucca's bayonets,
　　The mesquite's thorny maze.

The giant cacti guard him round
　　Like warders weird and grim,
And in the fading light afar
　　On yonder western rim,
Loom up in shadowy shapes that lift
　　Portentous arms to him.

He marks the crescent moon go down;
　　He sees the northern star
Rise o'er the verge, and lurid gleams
　　From mountain heights afar
Where savages by camp-fires brood
　　On deeds of death and war.

So speeds he on while sombre Night
　　Enfolds the mountains higher

With grateful veil till all is gloom,
  Save where the far-off spire
Of lofty Bab 'quivari lifts
  A finger-point of fire.

Oh, bless'd is night that brings respite
  From Sol's consuming glow,
Where ills beset the traveller
  More fell than savage foe,
And never the precious rain may fall,
  Nor cooling stream may flow!

Yea, bless'd to him who madly rides
  Beneath the dark'ning sky,
To cross the leagues of drouth and death
  That yet before him lie,
With eyes aflame, and blistered lips
  That tell of the canteen dry!

Yet forward under mortal need
  And duty's high demand,
Beyond the solemn noon of night
  He rides the lonely land,

Ringed with the soundless firmament
   And silent wastes of sand.

And now he reins his jaded beast
   Lest she be overdone,
For long the way, and desolate,
   Ere yet the goal be won,
And man and horse must drink or fall
   Before to-morrow's sun.

But if he reads the land aright,
   And all the signs that guide,
There lies a pool (of evil fame)
   Within an hour's ride
That must be sought and found to-night,—
   To-night whate'er betide!

Brief time he halts to mark his course,
   Where, looming in the West,
Grim El Diablo cleaves the sky
   With black, serrated crest,
And hides the darksome Devil's Well
   Within his rugged breast.

A pool ill-omened as the name
  By desert nomads given,
Yet unto many a hapless soul
  Athirst and frenzy-driven,
That black lagoon hath proven blest
  As benison from heaven.

But oh! a savage cul de sac,
  As desert legends tell!
Of murder foul and massacre,
  And tortures as of hell;
And men aver a savor still
  Of blood is in the Well!

Then on through narrowing defiles,
  Where mighty cliffs hung sheer
Above the rough and rubbled way
  He pressed in hope and fear,
Until his horse with sudden neigh
  Announced the water near.

And soon within embattled buttes—
  The birth of Vulcan powers

That ramparted a barren swale
  With splinter'd walls and towers—
He found the pool and camped thereby
  Until the morning hours.

A bowlder screened him from the wind
  That through the basin swept;
And while his broncho, tethered near,
  Sole guard and vigil kept,
And cropped the scanty grama grass,
  Her master soundly slept.

Yet waking once, he heard the beast
  Thrice whinny, as in fear;
She spied some hungry wolf, perchance,
  Or puma prowling near,
But never a sound of danger fell
  Upon his listening ear.

And so he turned to sleep again,
  As one would turn a page;
He only heard the night-wind's low
  Susurrus in the sage,

And eerie sounds of solitude
  There voiced from age to age.

And such the power of habitude,
  When need and suffering ceased,
Couched there within the sun-warm sand,
  Unfearing man or beast,
He slumbered sound as a cradled babe
  Till light broke from the East;

Then 'woke,—but not as sluggards wake,
  With yawn and drowsing air;—
Like warrior on the battle morn,
  Or wild beast in his lair,
He springs from sleep with faculties
  Full-armed to do and dare.

But who is here?—what presence this
  That greets his waking sight?—
A stranger at the Devil's Well
  Hath lodged near him o'er night,
And draped and huddled grimly sits
  Between him and the light!

Sits yonder by a bowlder braced,
  And swathed from top to toe
In tattered blanket, void of sign
  To mark him friend or foe,
Nor stirs,—it is the wind that waves
  The tatters to and fro!

Then rose the scout and searchingly
  The wrapt intruder scanned,
And, rifle poised, the summons sent—
  "Ho, stranger, show your hand!"
But never a sign the stranger gave
  To menace or demand.

Thereat, advancing warily,
  With battle in his eye,
Again he cried in louder voice—
  "Speak! stranger, or you die!"
But rigid yet the stranger sat
  Vouchsafing no reply.

Then to the muffled shape he strode,
  The wind-worn blanket raised;—

"A STRANGER AT THE DEVIL'S WELL"

There sat a grim and shrivell'd thing
    That held him horror-dazed!—
A semblance of himself that grew
    In likeness as he gazed!

Ay! in that stark cadaver there
    So shrunk and hollow-eyed,
His last, lost brother's lineaments
    Too surely he descried,
Whose battle wounds and riven scalp
    Bore witness how he died.

But hark! strange sounds arise, and see—
    The bristling yuccas stir!
The cacti shake,—away! away!
    Mount horse and drive the spur!—
The red fiends rise with shot and yell,
    And vengeful arrows whirr!

Like hounded panther forth he sprang,—
    But ah! e'en while he slept,
Strange hands had cut the lariat,
    And moccasin'd foes had crept

Between him and escape, and now
   From circling ambush leapt!

Then rose his courage with the need,
   The peril instant weighed,
And prone behind a hammock stretched,
   Such stern defence essayed,
That death flew hotly to the foe
   Around his barricade.

In vain, brave heart!—No single arm
   May vanquish a hundred foes!
And though beneath his deadly aim
   The savage life-blood flows,
From every rock and dune he sees
   The merciless circle close!

Then rang the Apache cry, and then,
   With simultaneous yell,
Down on that doomed and dauntless man
   Like famished wolves they fell,
And half a hundred eager blades
   Drank blood at the fateful Well!

* * * * *

A silence falls upon the hearth,
  And shadows darker grow
Where yet that aged mother waits,
  In piteous hope and woe,
The three brave sons who left her heart
  Such age-long years ago !

Still, day by day, her poor old eyes
  Peer out through the window-pane,
To watch the postman's daily round,—
  To watch, alas, in vain,
For tidings of the lost and dead
  That never shall come again !

INGERSOLL.

*"An atheist laugh's a poor exchange
For Deity offended."*—BURNS.

What doth the witty giber give,
   O fellow-mortal, unto thee?
Some golden rule whereby to live?
   Some anchor in futurity?
Nay, nay—not his the power
To lighten life or cheer one dying hour!

But words and mockeries are his,
   In lucre-seeking widely sown;
He saps belief with subtleties,
   And to the hungered gives a stone!
O soul, not of the scoffer
Seek thou what hope and faith alone can offer!

FLIGHT BEYOND FAITH.

Appalled I view the desolate goal
And triumph of the daring soul,
   That 'round his barren peak's eternal frost
Soars, eagle-like, in solitude of mind,
Beyond the genial faiths of all his kind,—
   To man's sublimest hope sublimely lost!

Seek ye that will, in wildering flights,
The deities of Olympian heights,
   Or chase the phantom lights beyond our line;
Enough for me the simple joys that grace
This blest and bloomful atom hung in space,
   To live in love, and die in hope divine.

DOUBT.

O Doubt, thou art the ruthless robber-chief
  That desolates our fanes and fairy lands!
  That murders Hope, and with remorseless hands
Destroys our precious hoardings of Belief,
Which but for thy grim wrack, O vandal thief,
  Had still supplied the hunger'd soul's demands!
  So now, like travellers whelm'd in desert sands,
Bereft our blessèd solacements of grief,
We toil forlorn o'er life's unbeaconed waste!
  Alas! the riches flown we may regain;
The shatter'd ship may haply reach the shore;
Lost loves and friendships all may be replaced:
  But one lost treasure we shall mourn in vain,—
O soul! thy vanished faith returns no more!

THE CREED OF HOPE.

Why question ye the deathless creed,
So sweet to all our mortal need,
So blest of highest thought and deed?

Or pridefully in judgment sit
On this and that of Holy Writ
To controvert or scoff at it?

Oh, blighting as the simoon's breath
To verdure is the voice that saith
The final goal of Life is Death!

Woe worth the Goth that would destroy
The simple faith—so fraught with joy!—
Of childhood in its tale and toy!

Or who would change our boon to bane
With bitter "Truth"—pronouncing vain
Our mortal cry to live again!

THE CREED OF HOPE.

Thy vaunted Truth is Dead Sea fruit!
Give Faith some pledges absolute
In her despoilment, or be mute.

Can Science tell us of the soul?
Nay—ask the darkly-delving mole
The problems of the Northern Pole!

Vain hope, alas, that e'er her scouts
Shall spy our future whereabouts,
And certify all hopes or doubts!—

That e'er her quest in earth and sky
Shall bring our hearts the full reply
To solace and to satisfy!

Life's mysteries lie thick about;
But oh, cast not contentment out
For vain half-knowledge, harrowing doubt!

Nor madly make a guide of one
Who, when his own faith-light is gone,
Cries from the darkness—"Follow on!—

THE CREED OF HOPE.

" Your systems teem with wrong and ruth,
And false your faiths and creeds, forsooth !
But follow ;—I have found The Truth ! "

Nor grope with the materialist
In pseudo-scientific mist
To prove that God doth not exist ;—

That dumb, insensate forces wrought
Dead matter into life and thought,
And marvellous systems—meaning nought !

Such myope only followeth
A mockery to doubt and death :
But farther-seeing broadens faith ;

And those star-measuring souls that soar
Beyond Orion's glowing core
See God in Nature, more and more.

He learns with loss who scans his bliss
Through microscopes, or tests a kiss
By ultimate analysis ;

What gives thee joy, and stirs the blood
And seemeth good—believe it good,
Nor doubt till all be understood.

Could ever trilobite foreken
The saurian, or such creature, then,
Thro' cycles vast see apes and men,—

Could ever embryo foresee
Its far evolvement—then might we
Have prescience of eternity,—

Behold through crude, incarnate vision
The coming marvels of transition,
The perfect soul and life elysian.

Yet, as the eaglet in his cell
Hath dreamful stirrings that foretell
His broader life beyond the shell,

So stirred are we; and so we say—
Thus far we fare upon the way
From darkened life to dawn of day.

How oft, bereft of blessèd sight,
Men walk at noon in utter night,
Unconscious of the glorious light!

The suns arise, the suns descend,
But, void the sense to apprehend,
Their lives are sunless to the end!

So, things that creep may ne'er descry
The vistas opening to the eye
And farther ken of things that fly.

And if some island-savage stand
Upon his sea-girt rim of sand
And say: "There is no other land,"—

To him there is no more;—to him
The sea-world stretches vast and dim,
And ends at the horizon rim.

His universe is what he sees,—
Scarce wider than the chimpanzee's,
In narrow round of tropic trees.

But light there is, though men may grope
In darkness, and to faith and hope,
Fair lands beyond the visual scope.

If from mere animalculum
This marvel grew—O Doubt, be dumb,
Nor idly gauge the growth to come!

Nor say, in Time's eternal flight
We cannot rise to higher height:
The powers unknown are infinite!

Since Nature's kindly alchemy
Restores in ways we cannot see,
The fallen leaf unto the tree;—

Since germs are quicken'd from the mire,
And lowly life hath mounted higher,
O Man, why may'st thou not aspire!

THE GOSPEL O' GAMMON.

ADDRESSED TO A SOCIALISTIC PREACHER.

I hear ye 've fought an unco' fight
Wi' ghouls that strangle Human Right,
Through grewsome shades o' doot and night,
    And wrang and ruth,
And find, at last, the bleezing light
    O' blessèd Truth.

In sic a cause, God speed ye, sir,
But, bonnie Truth—leuk weel at her!
For mony a glaikit worshipper,
    Syne Adam fell,
Has been her sole discoverer—
    As weel 's yersel!

And och! she 's proved a jinky jade
To countless devotees betrayed!

And mony a tragic escapade,
　　And hellish clamor,
Wi' faggot-fire and bluidy blade
　　Attest her glamour!

Ye may be wise, but O ye ken,
Fause lights hae dazed much wiser men!
And folk assert—and say 't again—
　　That ye 're pursuin'
A jack-o'-lantern ower the fen
　　O' moral ruin!

But is it true ye hae the plan
To equalize your brither man,—
End a' oppression, social ban,
　　And war and pillage,
And gie to each his bit o' lan'
　　For peaceful tillage?

And that ye merge in broader faith
The narrow creed o' Nazareth?—
Proclaiming, while sic want and skaith
　　Puir bodies bear,

We needna speer ayont the breath
    Hoo sauls may fare?

If true, guid sir, it is the chief
O' human gospel and belief!
Thraw up your hats, ilk tramp and thief,
    For creed sae canty!—
The Grace o' God is bread and beef,
    And Heaven is Plenty!

But, sir, sic change frae auld to new
May close the pulpit and the pew,
And ruin a' the preacher crew,
    I 've sair misgiving!
And what will puir auld Satan do
    To earn his living?

Sad thocht to grieve and gie us pain!
But loss is aft oor highest gain;
And when the De'il perceives hoo vain
    His auld pursuit is,
Hech, man! ye baith may then attain
    Mair useful duties!

Advice is aften oot o' place,
Yet, here 's a bit that fits the case :
If blether could redeem the race
    Your power is ample ;
But try the force o' Christian grace,
    And guid example.

Ye rail at Wealth wi' fine pretence,
While slave yersel to carnal sense ;
Ye eat the food of Opulence,
    And wear his raiment,
But frae the dole o' Indigence
    Exact the payment !

Ye ne'er hae lightened Labor's ways,
Nor eased Privation's dreary days
Wi' a' this reek and verbal haze ;
    But—De'il ma care !—
Ye gain what Toil to Gammon pays,
    If naething mair !

O souls, whase lot sae unco drear is !
Nae Babble-jack's ingenious theories,
And theologic whigmaleeries

THE GOSPEL O' GAMMON.

    Can gie relief,
Nor hush the harrowing misereres
    O' Want and Grief!

It 's nae in law to mend oor greeds;
It 's nae in catch-the-penny creeds,—
It 's nae in braw, new-fangled breeds
    O' priests and preachers,
To lift frae dool and grievous needs
    Oor fellow-creatures.

Self-seeking is the damning blot
Upon our happiness and lot,—
The ruling sin lang syne begot
    In Adam's fa';
Ye 'll find it in the peasant's cot,
    As weel 's the ha'!

And this, the universal shame,
Begrimes us a' wi' equal blame;
Sae, let us scan the way we came,
    And, faith! we 'll find
Reform maun rule in ilka hame
    To lift mankind!

PROGRESS—LIBERTY—DELUSION.

O, Progress! thou hast bred the greed
That grasps beyond our farthest need,—
  Runs riot through rich heritages
And robs the Earth of future seed!

Thy name inspires the madding host,—
Its shibboleth, its highest boast;
  And round the world the battle rages
Of Selfism, to the uttermost.

We waste the lands; we delve and plan
As if, forsooth, our little span
  Must compass all of man's achievement,
And nought be left to coming man!

Yea, in the name of Progress, we
Would sweep the Earth from sea to sea
  As with a locust plague and ravage,—
Despoiling all posterity!

And in the name of Freedom—lo,
The bomb and dagger, war and woe!
   Fawkes lives again,—the hissing fuses
Threat doom alike to friend and foe!

Peace! thou whose nature seems possest
With some dread spirit of unrest,—
   Whom frenzy leads, or base ambition,
To strike whate'er is wisest, best;

O rager at the common lot,
Who prates of Right and knows it not,—
   Who fires the evil blood of nations
With serpent tongue, assassin plot,—

Know, Leveller, by God's decree
While e'er an Alp o'er-tops the sea,
   Some men shall serve and some be sovereign;
The kingly soul the king will be.

Ne'er blight him with thy voice malign
Who toils content in field or mine;
   Nor quicken in him the restless devil
That murders Peace in hearts like thine!

Nor glorify this fevered reign
Of freedom thro' our fair domain,
  Till we have won content with freedom,
And wrought our lives to higher plane.

Though each of Nature's bounty shares,
And all have voice in State affairs,
  A fate austere adjusts the balance
With widening duties, wants, and cares!

So was it when that fateful pen
Proclaimed our helots equal men ;—
  New masters rose in needs despotic,
And forged their fetters o'er again.

But Freedom still (ye cry) is fair,
And ills that follow light to bear,
  Where merit wins exalted office,
And toiler ranks with millionaire.

Ay, so the Sirens sing to you
From Plymouth Rock, where we outgrew
  Old bonds and fled the old oppressors;
O God, that we could flee the new!

What boots it that our later lords
Rule not with mailèd hands and swords?
    Still thralls are we of venal masters,
Of babble-craft and Mammon hoards.

Alas, in our Utopian West,
Success howe'er attained is best!
    An arrant knave may wear the ermine,
And office-honor is a jest!

Behold the want, the greedy strife,
The office-hungry harpies rife,
    The slaughters, lynchings, strikes and riots,
The scorn of law and human life!

Wherefore these ills that Europe knows—
All crimes, all Misery's plaints and woes,—
    These crowded prisons, thronged asylums—
If human weal with freedom grows?

Nay, while we blare on every wind
The fallacies of men still bind,
    And cry the ballot-panacea
For all the ills that curse our kind,

The baser brood of equal rule
Degrades the family, State, and school,
  Sinks wise authority in chaos,
Exalts the ruffian, rogue and fool!

O peoples reared in greater stress,
How little of our lives ye guess!
  No happier we with larger bounty,
Nor is our sum of suffering less!

So learn with us, vexed souls afar—
Who deem our lot your guiding star—
  That happiness is not conditioned
On what we have, but what we are.

Beware the change not understood;
Beware the ills in guise of good;—
  The verbal guile and base self-seeking
That prompt to violence, hate, and blood!

HER DAYS OF JOY.

Adown the lane with beaming eye
    She hastens at the school-bell summons,—
A child-mind in a form well-nigh
    Full-statured as a woman's.

The glow of youth is in her flesh ;
    Her cheeks with robust health are redden'd ;
She looks on life with senses fresh,
    And feelings all undeaden'd.

And, as when in a theater
    On fairy scenes the curtain rises,
So Nature now unveils to her
    New pleasures and surprises ;—

Opes wide a wondrous world to view,
    As roseate as a morn in summer ;
And all seems bright, and pure, and true
    To this entranced new-comer !

Now from her winsome lips the song
　　Of inward joy spontaneous bubbles;
Now, garrulous with a weighty throng
　　Of childish thoughts and troubles,

Holds serious parley with herself
　　O'er problems grave;—a moment after,
With hop-and-skip, the wayward elf
　　Peals forth her merry laughter!

O happy girl! enjoy thy years
　　Of pleasance in this vale of glamour!
Long be thy woes but April tears
　　And puzzlements of grammar!

And heart-free from the worldly lore
　　That saddens life some period later,
Be thine the joys that bless no more
　　The wiser and the greater!

FRANK FORESTER.

[Lines written in a copy of "The Roman Traitor," found at a solitary miner's cabin in Grouse ravine, Sierra, California, 1881.]

O friend of yore, long lost to Life and Time !
Whose tragic fate in manhood's mellow prime
So grieved our hearts !—I meet thee here again
In this strong-living spirit of thy pen !—
Yea, in these forest solitudes that rise
On high Sierras to Hesperian skies,
Hear tuneful Æolus chanting in the trees
Thy own beloved " Cedars' " symphonies,—
As when, lang syne, in peace thou didst abide
By far Passaic's low-susurring tide !
For Nature speaks upon this Western verge,
From wood and mountain, desert sand and surge,
With self-same voice as where the airs of morn
Pipe through the Orient palms and day is born ;—
Brings unto him who climbs the alpine height,

Or cleaves with humming shrouds the polar
    night,—
Who sits 'neath English oaks, or lists the sound
Of canyon'd Colorado's gulf profound—
Some message from the ghostly crypts of yore,
Some touch of home and loved ones seen no more!

I tread with thee the forum and the camp;
Hear clash of arms and legionaries' tramp;
See in a Cicero attributes divine
A fiend incarnate in a Catiline,
And doughty Romans, famed in classic story,
Resurgent rise in all their shame or glory!

Through generations yet thy work shall plead
Sweet Virtue's cause to all who rightly read;
Shall show how joyless all, how vile and vain
The lives that yield to Passion's frenzied reign;
And how—tho' daring Heaven and Hell and
    Fate—
Guilt meets his doomful Nemesis soon or late!

God rest thee, friend! and whatsoe'er of fault
Thy sad life knew, rest with thee in the vault!

ENCHANTMENT.

Who harbors Love within his breast,
   Though born to toil and low estate,
Is by the glamour of his guest
Beyond the rich and high-born blest,
   And greater than the great.

The proud distinctions born of earth
   Are levelled at the rosy shrine;
Love knoweth nought of caste or birth ;
Love asketh only love and worth
   To bless with gifts divine!

O Love can ope the cottage latch
   To grander realm than ancient Rome !
And lift the lowly roof of thatch
With subtle sorcery, till it match
   Saint Peter's mighty dome!

IN ALTAS SIERRAS.

Once more, O hills sublime !
   For blest surcease of cares
   And sweet, inspiring airs,
Your peaceful heights I climb.

Here, from the haunts of men,—
   Out from the rutted lives
   And marts where baseness thrives,
I walk unthralled again.

My lordly pines once more
   Breathe welcome all and each,
   And loving arms out-reach
To him well known of yore.

Again, prone at your feet,
   I list the airy choirs
   Sing in your vernal spires
Old anthems grand and sweet.

And O! my spirit thrills
  With far-off sound that comes
  Like roll of muffled drums
From out the chasm'd hills;—

From canyon deeps profound,
  From gulch and river-bar,
  The roar comes faint and far
Of waters seaward bound,—

That icy bonds let loose
  To toil for miner hands
  In golden veins and sands,
In mill, and flume, and sluice,

Till flows each tawny flood
  With wreck of hills replete,
  But rich in future wheat,—
From ravage bearing good.

That sound hath brought again
  Through Time's encroaching haze
  The past, supernal days,
When life was young, and when,

With men strong-limbed and bold,
 I ranged this strange, new land
 To win with venturous hand
The Ages' garner'd gold ;—

What time the camp-fires gleamed
 On bar and mountain slope,
 And all with mighty hope
Of boundless treasure dreamed.

How sweet the simple fare!
 How sound the nightly rest!
 Was ever toil so blest,
Or life so free from care!

And when, with dam and wheel,
 We laid the bed-rock bare
 And spied the treasure there—
How rang our joyful peal

O'er Yuba's rushing tide!
 Yea, till each rocky shore
 Out-voiced his ancient roar,
And all the hills replied!

"HOW RANG OUR JOYFUL PEAL"

O peerless days no more!
  O mountains throned eternal!
  O forests vast and vernal!—
Where are the men of yore?—

The lion-hearted band
  That broke this solitude
  With shout and ravage rude,
With pick and axe and brand?

"Gone!" roars the yellow river;
  "Gone!" sigh the hills sublime,
  And "Gone!" the forests chime,
With solemn voice, "forever!"

Here, drowsing in the copse,
  I watch the dainty quail
  Trip shyly o'er the trail
With timid starts and stops;

Behold the startled hare
  Rise in the chaparral,—
  A great-eyed sentinel
Demanding, "Who goes there?"

And search with baffled sight
   The azure gulfs of sky,
   Whence comes the guttural cry
Of cranes in northward flight,—

That to the pilot bird
   Now singly make response,
   Now fanfare all at once,
As if his note had stirred

Some common memory then,—
   Perchance of pleasures shared
   When last they met and paired
By Borean lake and fen.

As higher yet I climb—
   Lo, mighty hills are knolls!
   And all the land unrolls
In billowy leagues sublime.

The forests halt and fail,
   Save where, beyond the lines,
   Some daring picket pines
Creep upward to assail

The citadels of frost;
   And now a hush profound
   Engulfs all separate sound,
And life and earth seem lost.

In solitude alone,
   In silence most intense,
   Breaks on the soul and sense
That mighty monotone

Beyond all power of word,—
   The deep, eternal bass
   Of Nature through all space,—
The voice of cosmos heard.

I stand in mute amaze,
   And reverent eyes upturn
   To icy peaks that burn
Beneath the solar blaze

As with celestial fires;—
   That stand like gods in scorn
   Of all things baser born,
And all earth-born desires.

O peaks majestical!
   Speak from your glorious heights!
   Inspire to noble flights
Souls prone to fail and fall,

Until they soar with you
   From all the moils below,—
   Pure as your driven snow,
In heaven's unsullied blue!

THE FINAL REBELLION.

Fair Earth seems foul with weeds
To you, alas, whose lives are narrowed in the
    gyves
  Of stern corporeal needs!

  To you whose prisoned souls,
As with a web of fate, strong-meshed and in-
    tricate,
  Grim Circumstance controls.

  The blessèd sunlight gleams
But dimly through your drear, aberrant atmos-
    phere,
  As in distempered dreams;

  And all the sweets of Earth—
God's bounty unto all—to some unfairly fall
  Who know not want or worth.

On you no fortune waits
With gifts not earned or just;—'t is yours to
    gnaw the crust
  Unknown beside her gates;

  Till, haply, strong to rise,
Ye breach with desp'rate lance the walls of
    Circumstance,
  And grasp her chary prize.

  But though ye may not reach
Good Fortune's rampart-wall,—though hapless
    myriads fall
  And perish in the breach,—

  Is this your neighbor's sin?—
The guilt of social law? Nay, friend, mayhap
    the flaw
  Lies nearer,—look within!

  There spy th' ignoble bent
That rules our selfish lives,—makes Lazarus
    grown to Dives
  A baser malcontent.

Not he who lords the soil,
But luxury and taste, false want, unthrift and
  waste
Keep us in bonds to Toil.

The fault is mine and thine;
For every willing hand may crop the liberal
  land
Of plenteous bread and wine,

But too gregarious grown,
And warped with cultured needs, ambitions,
  habits, greeds,
To nobler life unknown—

We turn with coward hearts
From Labor's peaceful lines, from prairie-lands
  and pines,
To moil in crowded marts,

And rutted channels tread,
Where throngs in frantic strife are narrowing
  hope and life
To Beggary's dole of bread.

Then, stirred by evil tongues—
That serve but to incite some mad crusade, or
    right
  Some wrong with greater wrongs—

  We hail the reckless rule
Of men who only seek to prey upon the
    weak
  And fatten on the fool;—

  Who sow the demon seed
Of chaos, claim the Earth for worthlessness and
    worth
  By equal title-deed,

  And prompt unbridled power
To raze the fabrics wrought through centuries
    of thought,
  In some phrenetic hour.

  No system in our ken,—
No law, can make us wise, or just, or equalize
  The diverse moulds of men,

Nor lift the laggard soul:
He who would rise and win must grow the
 power within,
Or miss his highest goal.

Equality 's a dream
Whene'er the word implies none o'er the mass
 shall rise,
No man may be supreme;

For his is all our gain,
Whom high, peculiar gifts, fair chance or fitness
 lifts
Above the common plane.

When men from lusts are free,
And none distinction seek,—when Chimborazo's
 peak
Is levelled to the sea,—

When toil hath equal yield
From rich and barren land, and all the wheat-
 ears stand
Full-level in the field,—

Then may your social plan,
O babblers, rule the Earth, and from unequal
worth
Uplift the equal man!

But, though some hands still reap
What other hands have sown, shall all be over-
thrown
And toppled to the deep?

Nay, though we splinter thrones,
Sweep Earth with sword and flame, we change
but in the name
Our despots and our drones.

And while our Sirens sing
The lullaby of fools—lo! frantic Demos rules,
Or Crœsus is the king!

Not thus shall justice come—
Not with the barricade and fratricidal blade,
With dynamite and bomb;

Nor shall privation cease
While swords still arbitrate, and reason yields
    to hate—
For Plenty comes of Peace.

Yet, ours the rebel's part:
Up, Rebels, then, and smite the nearest foes of
    Right
That lurk in every heart!

So let the fight begin,—
Put Self and Greed to rout, then shall the Earth
    without,
Grow fair to fair within!

IN MEMORIAM.

[Capt. Mathew Webb, the famous English swimmer, perished in the Whirlpool Rapids, Niagara, July 24, 1883.]

I.

O Niagara! what of him—
Sturdy-hearted, strong of limb,—
  Who, in such ill-fated hour,
For a transitory glory,
For a page in human story,
  Dared thy power,
And through raging rapids flying
Rued too late his rash defying?

Nought to thee, O black abhorrent,
Pitiless torrent,
  Is the Dead within thy keeping!
Nor the breaking hearts in Hull,
Nor the tears so pitiful,
  Wife and little ones are weeping!

Nought to thee the pigmy creatures
  That for profit, fame, or pleasure,
Come to view thy awful features,
    Creep around thy seething edges,—
Come to scan thee and to span thee
  With their puny human measure
    From the battlemented ledges!

Nay, though direst doom had hurl'd
All the millions of the world
  Into thy abysm,
And a universal woe
Wailed to Heaven from below,—
  Thou, O mighty cataclysm,
Still wouldst thunder!
Shaking all above and under,—
Stern as death and Nature's forces,
Void of mercies and remorses!

II.

Said the boatman, with a quiver,
  As he held his dory steady

On that mad, tumultuous river,
   For the swimmer, stript and ready—
(While the dory shook and trembled
With a terror undissembled!)
Said the boatman to the swimmer—
And his eyes grew strangely dimmer
   As he grasped the manly hand—
"Give it up, and come to land!
   O forego this mad endeavor—
      Think of children, think of wife!
   For I tell thee never, never—
Never yet passed living mortal
Through the Whirlpool's dreaded portal
      Breathing still the breath of life!"

But the swimmer shook his head,
   Sadly, as with grave misgiving;
—"*He who fears will fail*," he said;
Pressed the hand that fain had stayed him,—
Plunged from human power to aid him,—
   Plunged from all that joys the living,
To oblivion and The Dead!

III.

Daring swimmer, madly scorning
Timely warning,
And the loving heart that pleaded
All unheeded!—
In that last supreme endeavor,
Ere thine eyes were closed forever,—
 When thy limbs were in the toils,
And the deadly Whirlpool held thee
 Like a python in its coils,—
With the vision of despair
Through the fury-driven foam—
 Didst thou see an empty chair
In thy far-off English home?—
Did thy strong heart falter then,
 Seeing Love awaiting there
One who ne'er should come again?

IV.

Man of iron thews and will,
 Stranger to fatigue and fear,

All thy matchless strength and skill
   Failed thee here!
And thy story shall be written,—
"*He, the sturdy-hearted Briton,*
Who with dolphins might have sported,
Or consorted
With the sea-born Amphitrite—
Goddess mighty!—
He who, when the winds made frantic
The Atlantic,
Swam the Channel surges over,
Clear from Dover,—
In the deathful swirl and suction
Of thy maelstrom, O Niagara,
Met destruction!"

UTTERANCE OF THE DESERT.

If thou hast heard,
In Arizonan solitudes
And lonely lands unmastered yet of man,
The eerie swish and whisper of the wind
In all its moods
Through sage and cereus, till thy soul was stirred
With thought of Thought ere conscious life
    began,
And glimpsed the gulf Eternity behind
This prideful atom and his little span
That boasts the birth and boundary of mind,—
    Oh, then thy spirit caught
      The voice sublime
      Of utmost space and time,
And all that sound may syllable to thought!

    · And haply then—
    Far gazing o'er the desert sands,

Where, like a wraith of Hunger, travel-sore
The lean coyotè limps, and cacti lift
    Their wrinkled hands—
Thy fancy saw this deathful realm again
Re-peopled with the myriad life of yore,—
Heard murmuring multitudes in dune and drift
Recount the tale of Time for evermore,
Till thou didst question,—Was this wondrous gift
    Of mind inborn with man?
    Or did it live,
      A formless fugitive,—
Free tenant of the void since time began?

THE ETERNAL SIEGE.

Stern war is waged on every hand,
All round the world on reef and strand,—
The battle of the Sea and Land.

I stood at night where evermore
The great sea-dragons rush and roar
Snow-white with wrath upon the shore,

When, from the turmoil of the foes,
And thunder-shock of battle blows,
An overmastering voice arose;

As when profoundest forces shake
The earth till mountains roar and quake,
Thus to the Land the Ocean spake:

"I rage within thy seaward caves;
Thy headlands topple to my waves;
Thy islets sink in briny graves!

"Behold the doomful hieroglyphs
My surf's unbridled hippogriffs
Are carving on thy crumbling cliffs!"

Then from a vast portentous cloud,
That draped the hills with sable shroud,
A Land-Voice rumbled hoarse and loud:

"Vain boaster, cease! My rampart mocks
Thy rage through time and tempest shocks;
The centuries scoff thee from the rocks!

"These fertile fields,—yon blooming plain,
That waves its grateful sea of grain,
Are risen from thy dark domain;

"And these my mountains, that of yore
Thou didst engulf and triumph o'er,
Defy thee now for evermore!

"O robber Sea, thy boast is brief!
I master and despoil the thief:
Seest thou the rising coral-reef?

"There all thy wrath shall die in calms,
Thy thunders yield to drowsy psalms
Of tropic airs in cocoa-palms!"

The Sea (in scorn)—"Thy hopes are vain
As his whose weak, unbalanced brain
Outweighs grave loss with trivial gain.

"Prate not of centuries to me!
Time wields no sceptre o'er the Sea;—
Go babble to eternity!

"But Time is wearing thee apace,—
Yea, I behold thee shrink, I trace
The furrows deep'ning on thy face!

"O dotard!—never a stream may flow,
Wind blow, drop fall, nor flake of snow,
But leagues with me to lay thee low!

"Thus, might and Nature mark thee doomed!"
Awhile the sullen breakers boomed
Triumphant, till the Land resumed:

" To reason with the passion-blind
Is vexing to the balanced mind,
And vain as buffeting the wind.

" Thou wilt discern, when rage is spent,
Thy leaguers are my allies sent
To build the future continent.

" And vain, O Sea, thy vaunted might,
Who moves subservient day and night—
The vassal of a satellite ! "

As if a thousand cannon spoke
In simultaneous battle-stroke,
The thunder-shotted answer broke :

" Peace, slave ! The very worms that crawl
Upon thee hold thee basely thrall
But dread my potence, one and all;

" And though my humor it may please
To spare thy master-mite, and breeze
His cockle-fleets o'er friendly seas,

"No vassal to thy lord am I;
Who dares my sovereign will shall die!"
There was a pause, then came reply:

" A sovereign, sooth! Thou may'st o'erwhelm
Some hapless mariner at the helm
Who trusts him to thy treacherous realm;

"But, subject to the Master-hand,
The mite thou scornest holds command
As suzerain over Sea and Land.

" And though thou bury him from sight
In sunless caves where Death and Night
Keep vigil,—yet in thy despite,

" And Nature's, he shall live, I wot,—
Shall rise to his diviner lot
When thou, insensate Sea, art not!

" Yon sea-less orb within the skies—
Whose image on thy bosom lies—
Bids thee look up, reflect, be wise;

"In that drear moon, O Sea! behold
Thy own predestined fate foretold
When this fair Earth hath waxen cold

"Within her God-appointed place,
And sunward turns her shrivell'd face—
A cinder'd planet, dead in space!

"Like meagre cup to thirsty lips
Thou shalt be drained, till sunken ships
Uplift their spars from thy eclipse!"

There fell an instant hush, as when
In mortal onset warring men
Take breath for life or death,—and then

A terrible turmoil shook the Sea;
The billows rose prodigiously
And hurled their hissing spume to me.

The sea-mews, skurrying in affright,
Screamed thro' the black, tempestuous night;
The waves o'ertopped the beacon-light.

Then, while the battle-din rose higher,
I fled the scene so dread and dire,
And sought my peaceful hearthstone fire,

In faith that the Almighty Will
Decrees our final welfare still
Through Nature's utmost wrack and ill;

And walking forth at dawn, beheld
The foes yet warring as of eld,
Relentless, and with wrath unquell'd.

ON HEARING A DESERT SONG-BIRD.

O desert songster, piping clear!
How doth thy joyful carol cheer
This heart that fate hath banished here!

Such song, I ween, hath rarely stirred
These wastes, that erstwhile only heard
The croak of some ill-boding bird,

Or wolf-cry, or despairful wail
Of winds that breathe their eerie tale
O'er peak and bluff, and sandy swale.

O friend unseen! what chance or choice
Hath brought thee here with dulcet voice
To bid the wand'rer's soul rejoice?

Art thou, poor bird, an exile too,
From fairer lands where blossoms grew?
From loved ones, lost to heart and view?

Nay, nay, thine is a kinder fate
Than mine, for thou dost sing elate,
As one still happy with his mate!

And love so thrills thy little breast,
This barren realm 's an Eden blest
That holds thy lowly desert nest!

HIS EPITAPH:

TOM BLOSSOM, OF ARIZONA.

O mate, that roamed with me
  From Shasta's mighty shadow
  To where the Colorado
Down-thunders to the sea!—

Thou, tried as men are tried
  In regions wild and sterile
  Who meet the common peril,
By courage glorified,—

Now voiceless as the dead!
  O brave, ill-fated rover!
  If life's long tramp is over,
Be this above thee said:

"Here lieth one at rest
 Who paltered not, nor quailed,
 Whatever ills assailed,
But bravely did his best;

"Who, true to every friend,
 Met squarely fate and foe,
 Met frontward every blow
Unflinching to the end!

"And triumphs o'er the past;
 For though the earthly treasure
 Ne'er blessed him, who shall measure
The prize he gains at last!"

NIGHT-FALL ON THE YUBA.

On yon Sierras' high embattled crest,
The dying Day looks fondly from the west;
And lo! the rugged buttes in glory loom—
Far, blessèd isles upon a sea of gloom,
Whose black and soundless tide, upwelling higher,
Engulfs anon the summit's lingering fire.

Full soon the rising anthem of the pines
Drowns all the stir of far-down camps and mines;
The sharp, assiduous axe is stilled at last;
The crash of timber and the sullen blast
Shock earth no more, and but the river peals
His resonant roar, with shriek of miners' wheels.
All sounds of life grow fainter with the light,
Till Nature's voice pervades the hush of night.

NIGHT-FALL ON THE YUBA

Gleams through the curtain'd gulf a tawny
  thread,
Where brawls the Yuba o'er his rocky bed:
The solemn diapason of his flow
Thus rose and fell ten thousand years ago!—
Nay, through undreamed eternities of years,
Resounded thus unheard of living ears!

O Yuba! who shall measure thy abyss
With gauge of Time?—declare the genesis
Of that first feeble rill, whose gathering force
Carved on the seaward slope thy wayward course,
Through cycles deepening under ceaseless law
By flood and avalanche, by frost and thaw,
Till thus, through mountains cleft to misty deeps,
Now seen, now lost, thy sinuous torrent sweeps?
Not thou, O man! for on this brink sublime,
One pendulum beat counts all historic time;
Here shrinks thy day and record unto nought,
Where awful Age looms visible to thought!

No chance catastrophe, no sudden shock,
Broke way through these abysmal miles of rock;

Here Nature worked in calm, majestic ways,
Nor haste nor passion knew, nor lapse of days.
Her seeming wrath, tho' fraught with dire
    distress,
Is fury only to our feebleness,
That broader growth in knowledge of her law
Shall make benignant, and divest of awe.
As stern as we, whose casual touch and breath
Are grewsome shocks or hurricanes of death
To tiny creatures,—storms calamitous
To life unseen as Nature's are to us.
A falling leaf destroys the spider's bridge;
A rain-drop proves a maelstrom to a midge,—
Yea, life may perish if a zephyr blow—
Such trifles whelm the little! Even so
To giant beings of some farther sphere
Might seem the powers that most appall us here.

So she that knows not Time, with patient will
Wrought here the gorge and reared the mighty
    hill,—
Gnawed down by age-long inch thy rocky bed,
O Yuba, while thy torrent seaward sped;

Till, from the stubborn matrix shattered loose,
A stream of gold bestrewed thy mighty sluice,—
The last residuum holden from the sea
Of comminuted mountains borne through thee;
A gift beyond the dream of Avarice
From lost, primeval ages unto this,
And spied but yesterday.—When fled thy reign,
O Solitude! and o'er this wild domain—
Where, erstwhile, sounds of elemental war,
The land-slip's thunder and the torrent's roar,
The scream of eagle vaulting down the sky,
The owl's grave note, the puma's thrilling cry,
Alone stirred Echo from his ancient lair—
Brake suddenly upon the startled air,
The clamor of a strange, unwonted strife,
And hither flowed, in frenzied streams of life,
The late-come beings that overswarm the globe,
Make Nature vassal and her secrets probe.

Here, where the mountain buttress grandly
    sweeps
From sunlit summits sheer to sunless deeps;—
Where skulks the grizzly, and the hare and quail

Unfearing haunt the seldom-trodden trail,
That through the matted manzanita opes
A devious way to higher, bleaker slopes;—
Where evermore, from streams and forest-seas,
Rise solitude's eternal symphonies,—
Scarp'd in the lofty ridge's narrow crest
A human frame hath found its final rest.

Long fallen lies the rude-built cairn of stone,
By winds and forest prowlers haply strown;
The shattered head-board crumbles in decay;
All record of the dead hath passed away.
Yet he may live in memory;—some may weep
For this lone tenant of the weather'd heap,—
Reach hands imploring toward the western sun
For sign of him ere ebbing life be done!

Though of his name and nation, life and death,
No tongue doth tell, no record answereth,
Yet, to the musing eye this much is shown:
He was a man, to man's full stature grown
When only men of strong, adventurous mould
Here led the van in strenuous quest of gold.

He came, perchance, as those forerunners came,
To spy new lands, with golden dreams aflame;
Perchance embitter'd by some social ban,
Fled here to Nature from his fellow-man,
And in the strife with Nature, or in strife
With man more stern, untimely closed his life.

There is a pathos in these relics here
To stir the spirit and invoke a tear;
For kindly Pity turns the human heart
To all who strive and fall, and lie apart,
In ways remote, in ocean's sounding caves,
Beyond humanity in lonely graves!
Oh, not yet lost to us are ye that lie
Beneath the sea or under alien sky!—
On Mexic plain, in deadly Darien swamp—
In desert sands, or far Nor-western camp!
Nor you, brave hearts, long battling for the goal,
Whose icy barrows guard the fateful Pole!

But sorrow not for him who takes his rest
So grandly urned on this Sierran crest;

For what were organ-peal and cannon-boom,
The pageantry of woe, the blazon'd gloom
Of vaulted abbey and imperial tomb,
Or all the burial pomp the great secure,
To this Unknown's majestic sepulture!
Nay, every child of Nature here would cry—
As thus inurned he lieth, let me lie,
'Mid hymning pines, and vaulted with the sky!

Day's after-glow departs from yonder west,
And warns away, O Dead, thy living guest!
The far lights beckon, and he takes again
The downward trail to travell'd ways of men.
Good-night to thee, O Nameless of the height!
He leaves thee here to Solitude and Night,—
For yet life's duties call; when these are o'er,
He would return and journey hence no more.

THE END.

1

www.ingramcontent.com/pod-product-compliance
Lightning Source LLC
Chambersburg PA
CBHW020255170426
43202CB00008B/380